MONTH-BY-MONTH
Arts & Crafts

MARCH · APRIL · MAY

Compiled and Edited by Marcia Schonzeit

SCHOLASTIC
PROFESSIONAL BOOKS

New York · Toronto · London · Auckland · Sydney

To my son Sam,
a swell cutter and paster.

Designed by Nancy Metcalf
Production by Intergraphics
Illustration by Terri Chicko, Joe Chicko, and Stephanie Pershing

Cover design by Vincent Ceci
Cover photography by John Parnell

ISBN 0-590-49125-3

CONTENTS

MARCH 7

All of March brings cause for celebration—it's National Youth Art Month! "There's no one quite like you" is the message conveyed through self-portraits, personalized stationery, and creative crafts of all kinds.

APRIL 29

Experience springtime flower power! Set the scene with mobiles, stencils, collages, 3-D paper sculpture, and more. Paper blossoms in colorful and creative projects for Arbor Day and National Library Week too.

MAY 49

A tisket, a tasket, May baskets and garlands! Other project ideas include abstract designs and delicate wire sculptures as well as cards and gifts to celebrate Mother's Day. Then decorate year-end classrooms with flower chains and individual memory hangings.

Using This Book in Your Classroom

Month-By-Month Arts & Crafts offers you more than 50 classroom-tested, illustrated suggestions for every month of the school year. Because most of these projects were submitted to *Instructor* magazine by teachers just like you, you'll find them teacher friendly, success oriented, and appealing to a wide range of ages and abilities. Designed to promote individual creativity, the activities will please you as well as your students. Keeping in mind the needs of today's classroom, these arts-and-crafts experiences rely on inexpensive, easy-to-obtain materials. The emphasis is on simplicity, minimal fuss, and the fun of creating.

The activities, categorized by month, range from fresh-as-the-breeze ideas to welcome windy March to delightful Mother's Day suggestions in May. Seasonal projects celebrate major holidays and highlight other special events every month. In addition, there are ideas for bulletin-board displays and class projects as well as opportunities to experiment with such techniques as collage, papier-mâché, painting, puppetry, and drawing.

Many of the projects also integrate other curriculum areas. Drawing a symmetrical design, for example, or making an inchworm ruler involves mathematical concepts. Having students tell a story about their drawing establishes a language-arts link. And social studies tie-ins occur naturally as part of activities that celebrate birthdays of inventors, presidents, and other national figures. Scientific principles are implicit in designing windsocks or creating pictures with magnetized filings.

A resource section on page 70 suggests background information and sources of inspiration to spark projects from paper folding to assembling collage compositions and quilting with traditional designs. Finally the index presents activities in alphabetical order, with special listings for major holidays.

Evaluating an arts-and-crafts project is no longer limited to judging whether or not a child is "good" at art. More important is the expression of each child's unique view of the world. Experiencing the joy of seeing and the pleasure of creating are goals worth encouraging. Through these projects children learn to experiment without worrying about the "right" answer. They learn to expand their imagination. And they learn nonverbal ways to express themselves.

You may want to establish a link between school and home. A reproducible Letter to Parents on page 6 of this book enables you to enlist help from home in assembling scrap materials of all kinds. After your students have completed the activities in each of the *Month-By-Month* books, invite parents to an exhibition of the children's projects. Involve the class in displaying the artwork, taking home invitations and conducting tours through the gallery. Encourage home displays, too, with holiday gifts and other take-home ideas.

We hope that *Month-By-Month Arts & Crafts* provides you and your students with many hours of creative pleasure.

Letter to Parents

Teachers, you may want to make copies of this letter and hand them out to your students during the first week of school. You can save time and paper by highlighting the objects you need as the projects come up. Remind your students to return the letter with the material from home. Place the letters in a file until you're ready to send them home again. Don't write any names on them—that way you can redistribute them.

Dear Parent:

We need your help!

Our class needs the following items for our arts-and-crafts projects. Please start saving them now, and I'll let you know when we'll need them.

<u>Due Date</u>

1. paper towel rolls
2. toilet paper rolls
3. magazines
4. soup cans
5. pieces of cloth, fabric scraps
6. ribbons, yarn, string, rope
7. cardboard boxes
8. old greeting cards
9. paper plates
10. wire coat hangers
11. clean Popsicle sticks
12. other:
13. craft materials you'd like to share with us:

Thanks,

MARCH

Greet windy March with colorful kites, a wind-sock project, and a jaunty parachutist. Look ahead to spring with activities that feature flowers and butterflies, even a soft sculpture March lion and lamb.

And there's fun for all on St. Patrick's Day with clever shamrock prints, puppets, masks, and mobiles.

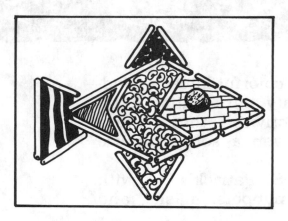

Fish Collages

Using lengths of straws, students outline fish forms on pieces of poster board and glue them in place with clear-drying white glue. Children decide what kind of texture and design they want and glue an assortment of beans, noodles, pebbles, black-eyed peas, bits of paper, cardboard, and other materials onto the shape. A decorative button or round piece of cork might make an eye, and a strip of colored foil a body stripe.   Verdie F. Adams

Self-Portraits

Fold a piece of 12- by 18-inch white drawing paper into four equal sections to make a standing rectangle. Have students analyze their features in a mirror, then draw a self-portrait from all four views. Ask them to capture hair style, face, nose shape, and eye color. When the portrait is finished, tape the inside edges so it will stand.   Minnie Knych

• *Looking for a good reason to celebrate March? It's National Youth Art Month!*

Cross-Stitch Creation

Use graph paper as a guide for stitching on plastic foam trays. Cut your graph paper to the size of the tray, tape it down, and "X" in your design on the paper. Using a blunt-ended needle and fine yarn, stitch right through the paper and the tray. Carefully pull away the graph paper when you are finished, removing any pieces stuck under the stitches with the end of the needle.   Jane Charland

Food Mobiles

Familiarize your class with the different kinds of fruits and vegetables. (You may be surprised to find out the number they do not know.) If possible, prepare small pieces of those that are good to eat raw and pass out samples. Show colored pictures from nursery and seed catalogs. Children can cut out and hang colored-paper shapes of their favorites from coat hangers or similar armatures. Food shapes can be made eight-sided, as shown.

Flower Magnets

Make floral refrigerator magnets from construction paper, a tongue depressor or Popsicle stick, and a magnet. Have children cut out flower petals from construction paper and arrange them in an overlapping flower pattern. Attach the petals to the stick, affix a magnet to the back of it, and the flower is ready to give as a gift. Sallie Speights

Personalized Stationery

Put your fingerprints on your own stationery and greeting cards! Use a regular washable-ink stamp pad; or make your own pad by cutting several layers of felt to fit an old jar lid, then saturating the felt with washable ink or thin tempera paint. Press your thumb or fingertip on the pad, then on the paper. Use colored pencils, ballpoint, or felt-tip pen to add lines that change your print into an object, a figure, or an animal. Adding eyes, beaks, claws, noses, legs, and tails makes the possibilities endless. You can even place two or three prints next to each other for figures with heads and bodies.

Painting With Bleach

Substitute bleach for paint and a cotton swab for a paintbrush to create exotic-looking drawings. Working on 9- by 12-inch sheets of construction paper, students dip the cotton swab into a small cup of household bleach, then draw with brushlike strokes. Encourage children to create details and patterns. Sometimes two applications of bleach will be necessary to fully lighten the original color. Dark colors offer good contrast, but black will not work. Allow about 10 minutes for the bleach to take full effect.

Now color the unbleached areas with crayon, leaving some background paper showing. Are you studying Mexico or India, or the sphinxes of Egypt? This inexpensive process will bring the stylized animals and statues of those countries' art to life.

Marla Kantor

Wool Paintings

This South American folk art is easily reproduced by students. To begin a wool painting, have students draw a design on cardboard in pencil. The design should be kept simple and full of large shapes. Then have students apply glue directly to the cardboard design and press pieces of bright woolen yarn into place, making sure all spaces are filled. If necessary, hold the yarn in place with pins until the glue dries. After the paintings are finished and dry, they can be mounted under a sheet of pre-cut Plexiglas to keep them from getting dirty and for permanent display purposes.

Liesa Schroeder

Everyday Objects

As children become older, they have a strong desire to "draw it the way it is." This is a good time to work on strengthening drawing skills. Do this by using familiar objects as models. Have children touch, hold, and feel everyday gadgets and containers. Ask them to shut their eyes and try to "draw" images in their minds. Try having them use the eraser ends of pencils to make simple outline draw-ings. They can try this with their eyes closed and then again with them open. After examining their eraser sketches they can brush away incorrect sections, correct them, and follow the faint eraser lines with markers or brush and ink. Open areas can be painted with washes of color. Texture can be added by using crayons or pastels.

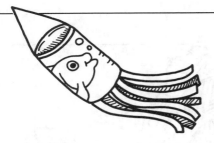

March Windsock

Give each child a 12- by 18-inch sheet of construction paper. Decorate with colored markers. Glue six 2- by 12-inch strips of colored tissue paper to the bottom edge of the construction paper. Roll the paper into a cylinder and fasten edges together with glue. Next, punch two holes through the top on opposite sides. Cut a 12-inch length of yarn and knot ends securely at each hole. (Do not thread yarn through the holes.) Hang students' windsocks near the classroom window to catch the spring breeze.   Donna A. James

Positive-Negative Design

Cut a simple design from black paper, then cut the reverse of the design from light-colored paper. Paste them opposite each other on another paper so the designs appear to be reflections. Continue alternating layers of contrasting colors to make the designs more intricate.   Sister Gwen Floryance

Clever Kite

Fold a 9- by 12-inch paper in half lengthwise. Cut out a large triangle, with the base at the fold. Cut out two smaller triangles from inside the first. Open, glue tissue to the back, add a yarn tail, and decorate.
Eleanor DeJulio

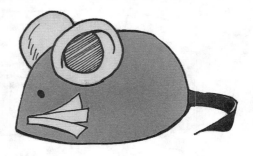

Folded-Paper Mouse

Fold a piece of construction paper in half, and cut a semicircle for the mouse's body. Leave top uncut and have tabs at base extend 3/4 inch. Fold both base tabs inward and glue together. Now glue sides together. Glue on cutout eyes, whiskers, and tail. To make ears, cut two pink paper circles and glue inside cup-shaped plastic packing pieces. Glue on mouse's head.
Joyce C. Davis

Whole-Figure Stick Puppets

Draw, color, and cut out any figure or object. It might be a person, animal, bird, car, train, or such objects as houses, chairs, or trees to depict scenery. Paste the shape on heavy cardboard or oak tag and cut out. Tape or glue the stick on the back. Magazine pictures also can be used to create quick puppets.

Colors That Dance

Using only colored paper, scissors, and glue, Matisse made figures and whimsical shapes that dance across museum walls. Look at some of Matisse's cut-paper collages. Have students decide which colors and shapes they want to work with, do a bit of planning, and help them use their scissors to "draw" their own shapes from their paper. Encourage students to move the shapes around on the background until they are happy with the composition.

With older children, practice cutting out figures from black paper. Children may need to use pencils to draw figures first and practice cutting different poses in silhouette form, though some may find it easier to cut a figure out freehand in silhouette form. Have each child choose at least three different poses for his or her collage. Glue these to colored paper or make one big classroom mural.

Marla Kantor

• *See page 70 for source materials to use with collage projects.*

Parachute Pictures

To make the parachute, draw a scalloped line down the center of a plastic foam dessert plate. Cut the plate along the line. Cut lengths of white string. Fasten the pieces of string at regular intervals along the scalloped edge of the plate with masking tape. Staple the plate to a piece of construction paper with the strings hanging toward the bottom of the paper. Gather the string bottoms together and glue down to the paper. Draw and cut out a person in parachuting clothing. Glue the person over the glued-down string ends.

Beatrice Bachrach Perri

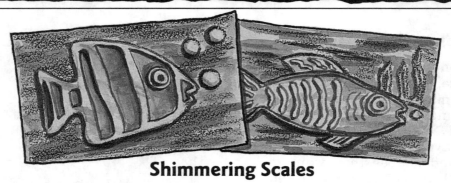

Shimmering Scales

Shining metal repoussé fish designs are almost as dazzling as real goldfish in a dark pond. Wooden pottery tools, a thick magazine or newspaper cushion, tooling foil, and markers are the materials needed for this project. First, sketch designs on paper the same size as foil. Remember that final compositions must be simple and large enough to facilitate the pressing technique used with repoussé. Place completed sketches on top of cushioned foil and trace, indenting metal slightly. Work from *back* of metal and press main shapes into cushion by rubbing gently with tools. When foil is turned over, these shapes will stick out in relief. Keep turning foil from back to front, to see where you need to press. Press evenly to avoid wrinkles and folds. As designs are completed, add texture by placing pieces of paneling and bumpy plastic sheets under foil and rubbing. Color with markers when finished. Be sure to leave some surfaces without color.

Verdie F. Adams

Clothespin Butterflies

To make these beautiful butterflies you'll need clothespins, pipe cleaners, coffee filters, and an eyedropper. First add several drops of food coloring to a small amount of water. Then use the eyedropper to release drops of the mixture onto the coffee filter. Let dry. Gather the filter in the middle and attach the clothespin. Feed the pipe cleaner through the opening at the top of the clothespin and twist to make the butterfly's antennae.

Tammy Woodel

Pussy Willows

Pussy willows tell everyone that spring is on the way! Draw or paint branches on construction paper. Saturate small sponges with gray tempera paint to use as stamp pads, and let students' fingertips make the individual catkins.

Kathleen Polaski

Ladybugs

Use a 9-inch paper circle for the ladybug's body. Students draw a "v" down the middle of the circle with black crayon. Then they color in large black dots on the circle and fill in the spaces around the dots with red crayon.

Then cut four slits in the circle.

Tuck down piece between each slit, fold over the outer pieces and staple in place. Roll pieces of black construction paper and glue them onto the body for eyes. Staple black pipe cleaners above the eyes for antennae. Punch a hole in the front of the ladybug and attach a string so students can "walk" their ladybug.

Dee Le Fevour

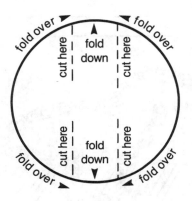

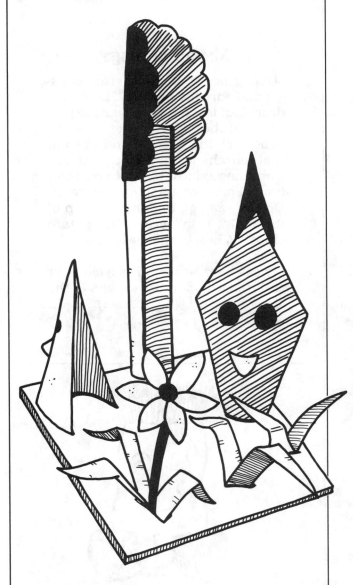

3-D Paper Sculptures

Cover a 6- by 9-inch piece of cardboard with a piece of construction paper for a base. Students use construction paper and glue to make a three-dimensional sculpture. They cut shapes and figures from construction paper and glue them to the cardboard base. Encourage creativity and let students experiment with shapes and sizes.

Joel A. Nelson

Shopping Bags

Use grocery bags as the background for this project. Have children decide what they want to purchase at the supermarket.

Then let them draw and cut out their purchases (or cut out pictures from magazines) to paste on their bags. Focus on packing the items. Do the eggs go under or on top of the milk? Don't crush the potato chips! Where's the best place for cans?

These bags are good recyclers for children and parents to take to the store.

Susan Rodriguez

Potato Friends

Each child draws a face on a potato, using permanent markers, pins on a green bow. Cut off potato tops and bore a small hole in each one. Place a ball of moist cotton inside the hole. In a week, heads will grow crew cuts.

Sandy Campion

Pop-Top Art

Pull-tabs from cans of soda are arranged without predrawn lines. Heavy clear-drying glue holds them in place. Cut or torn construction paper forms horizon.

Sister Gwen Floryance

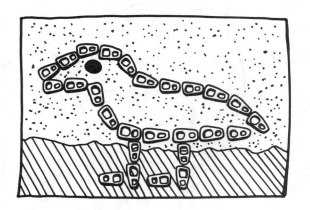

Color Thermometers

This color exercise for all ages uses tempera paint to create color thermometers. Help children *feel* the temperature of colors by asking them to think about winter and which colors are cool, refreshing, minty. Which colors do they think are hot and fiery?

Cut paper into long strips (about 6 inches by 18 inches) and write *hot* at the top, then *warm, cool,* and finally *cold* at the bottom. After children have the feel for color temperatures, painting can begin.

Decide which colors go where on the strip. Paint can be mixed in egg cartons or directly on the paper. Children may want to practice blending colors into each other. Display the finished thermometers. Let children discuss their feelings about the colors and share their blending and mixing techniques.   Marla Kantor

• *See page 70 for source materials to expand a lesson on color.*

Colorful Collage

Pick any animal and color that start with the same consonant and create a wonderful "animalage." On the simple cutout shape of the animal attach a grand array of collage materials in the selected color. Finish with the large cutout letter you are illustrating. (Examples: G for green giraffe, P for purple puppy.)   Joan Lunich Schenk

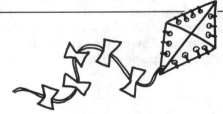

Stuffed Paper Kite

Place two pieces of construction paper on top of each other. Cut out a kite shape. Then punch holes approximately 1/2 inch apart around the perimeter of the kite with a hole punch. Sew the kite shapes together with a piece of yarn. Add stuffing inside the kite (newspaper, tissue paper, scrap paper, etc.) before making final stitches. Tie a knot at the bottom of the kite. Allow excess yarn to dangle down for the tail. Add pieces of paper to tail for decoration. Hang kite from ceiling to catch the breeze.

Carolyn Martin

Tube-Sock Hand Puppet

Make a slit across the toe of a tube sock. Cut a circle of red felt and sew or glue in the opening of the sock to make an open mouth. Add button eyes, stitchery eyelashes, other details. Slip the sock over your hand and arm; open and close the mouth by manipulating fingers. Fingers fit in the top of the mouth, thumb in the chin.

Fanned-Out Flower

Fold four pieces of 6- by 9-inch construction paper accordion-style so the folds are 9 inches long. Scrunch together one end of the fan and staple it together to hold the fan shape. Staple the four fans together at the bunched ends to form the four quadrants of the flower. Cut a center for the flower from construction paper and glue over center of flower to hide place where quadrants are joined together. Staple flower to an oaktag background. Add a stem of construction paper and a flowerpot cut from old scraps of fabric, wallpaper, etc.   Joan Mary Macey

Magnetic Plaques

With a few different types of magnets and some iron filings, children can not only discover the mysterious lines of force around a magnet but have an interesting art activity as well. Place a magnet or magnets on a flat surface, in interesting designs. Lay plain white paper over them, and slowly sprinkle filings until the magnetic fields appear. Spray them with a clear acrylic spray. When the spray hardens, it fixes the filings to the paper. Make a display for your bulletin board or hallway with these finished works of magnetic art. They are especially effective against a brightly colored background.   Philip Pankiewicz

Party Hat!

Reminder: Use absolutely square paper. When first folding, letter both sides of the paper to correspond to the lettering in the diagram. 1. Position paper with point A at the top, and fold point A to point C. 2. Fold point B to point D and reopen. This gives you center point E. Fold point D to A, placing fold ED on centerline EA. Repeat with B. 3. Bring points B and D up to E, creating fold FG. 4. Fold points B and D forward along line HJ and IJ. 5. B and D are now slanting triangular flaps. 6. Pull point A upward. Place between flaps on centerline. Fold KL. 7. Fold along FG, bringing KL up and above FG. 8. Turn hat over and fold C to point E or reverse fold and tuck inside. *Party Hat is taken from* Papercrafts *by Ian Adair (David and Charles Holdings Ltd., 1975).*

• *See page 70 for books that include other paper-folding projects.*

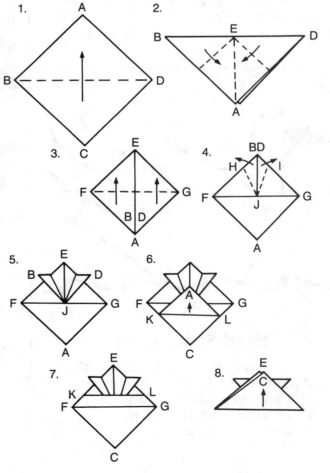

Lion and Lamb

Cut out a front and back for each animal from cloth. Sew together, then stuff with tissue. Stiffen limbs with cotton swabs. Curl paper for the lion's mane. Decorate.

Barbara Ellis

Magazine Mansions

Each child cuts a basic house shape from large paper. Chimneys, porches, and other "extras" can be part of the shape or added later. Next, students select pictures of individual rooms from home-decorating magazines; last of all they cut and paste in more furniture and decorative details and touch up with markers.

Helen Kratcha Thomas

Hand-Some Swan

Children trace around hands with fingers together and thumbs extended. They add eyes and beaks to the thumbs and tack the shapely swans to a bulletin-board "pond."

Linda Wong

City Night Scene

On black construction paper, paste paper building cutouts. Add windows and doors. Use a variety of materials to create scenery—cotton clouds, stick fences, a foam moon.
Sister Gwen Floryance

Symmetrical Butterflies

Make these beautiful butterflies with the same technique used to make symmetrical hearts. Fold a large piece of construction paper in half and draw and cut out the shape of a butterfly. Then fold smaller pieces of construction paper of various colors. Cut out different interesting shapes. Cut each shape along the line of symmetry so there are two shapes. Glue each one onto corresponding locations on both sides of the butterfly.

Joel A. Nelson

Peanut Creatures

Let children experiment gluing peanuts together in different and unusual animal shapes. Paint with fluorescent colors and use glass beads or paper-punch dots for eyes. Paint or draw suitable backgrounds for the nutty menagerie, then display.
James Perrin

- *Don't forget—March is National Peanut Month!*

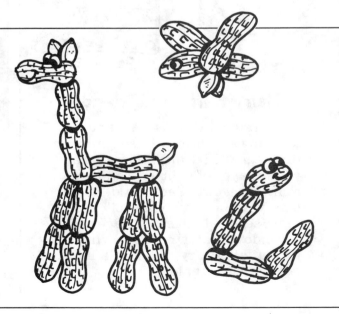

Ichabod Inchworm Ruler

Follow a lesson on measurement with an opportunity for children to make a folded-paper "inchworm" ruler. (For metric measurement lessons, make a Maizie Metric Ruler. Simply mark the strip in centimeters, using a metric ruler as a guide.)

On a narrow strip of paper, mark inches and half inches, using a regular ruler for a guide. Stress the importance of accuracy. Fold inches up, accordion-style, and paste head behind first inch. To make rulers more durable, run several strips of cellophane tape along them. Or use strips of transparent adhesive-backed plastic.

Hairy Harry and Friend

Decorated tin cans can add an amusing touch to a lesson in soil drainage. Fill Hairy Harry's can with a layer of pebbles, sand, and rich loose dirt. Pack Bald Bert's can with a clay-type soil. Sow grass seed in both cans. Place near a window, water regularly. In no time at all, Harry will need a haircut. Bert stays bald.

Windy-Day Kites

Make tiny kites from toothpicks, tissue paper, and yarn tails. Glue kites to a sky-blue background and complete the picture with cotton-ball clouds, twig and tissue-paper treetops, and construction-paper roofs.

Sandpaper Prints

Have children draw bright crayon pictures on fine sandpaper. Cut lightweight drawing paper the same size as the sandpaper and place it over the drawing. Iron with an iron set on medium (an adult should do this) until crayon shows through the back of the paper. Because of the roughness of the sandpaper, the resulting picture will look as if it has been painted with dots, reminiscent of the work of the impressionist painter Seurat.

Laura Dickinson

Floating Shamrocks

Let March winds move an airy shamrock mobile! Cut one shamrock. (Shamrocks are three hearts together, you know.) Then suspend three smaller ones from it with strong thread. Use samples of wallpaper to cut printed motifs; paste on the basic shamrock shapes.

Sister Gwen Floryance

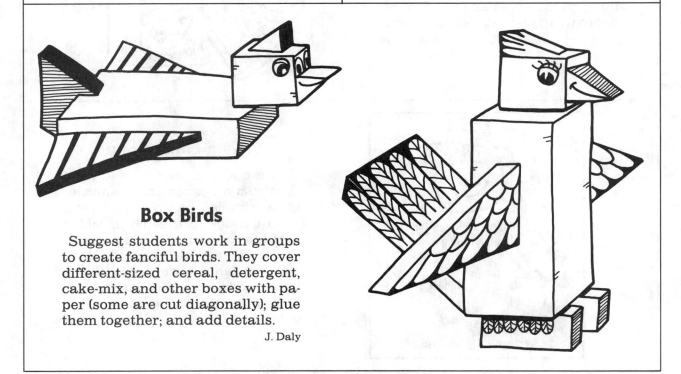

Box Birds

Suggest students work in groups to create fanciful birds. They cover different-sized cereal, detergent, cake-mix, and other boxes with paper (some are cut diagonally); glue them together; and add details.

J. Daly

Tater Shamrocks

Cut raw potatoes in half and draw a small shamrock on each section. Cut away outside so shamrocks are about 1/2 inch high. Make a stamp pad by cutting felt to fit a shallow lid and soaking it sparingly with tempera. Students use potato shamrocks to make designs.
Kathleen Allan Meyer

Cereal-Box Masks

Remove one end and back or front of box. Cover with green paper. Determine where eyes and mouth of wearer are and make holes in box. Use different paper to design shamrock petals. Trim with bulky yarn, more paper, and paint. Attach yarn ties to fasten masks.
Mark Shed

Love a Leprechaun

Have children tear a head from construction paper and then color in a simple, happy face. Next choose shades of green from which to tear a hat and clothes, and paste all on oak-tag background. Have children add torn-paper hands, shoes, and accessories such as buttons, a beard, and even a pot o' gold!
Jan Shay

A Touch of Irish Lace

Irish ancestors or not, try using bargain lace to trim "family" portraits. Twist colored tissue paper into noses and a mouth. Add a bit o' bulky yarn for hair and a bow. 'Tis 3-D art you've created! And a happy sight it is!

Pat Lang

Leprechaun Puppet

This stick-puppet leprechaun can dance an Irish jig or pop out from behind a shamrock whenever the mood strikes him! On a lightweight piece of cardboard, draw a leprechaun wearing a jaunty green hat. Cut out the shape and glue on a red yarn beard and fabric-scrap clothes. Make a staff from a green pipe cleaner topped with a tiny paper shamrock. Glue a Popsicle stick to the back and get set for some St. Paddy's Day fun. Tom Rose

Green Grass Shamrocks

Draw a shamrock shape on the chalkboard. Give each child a small sponge to cut into this shape. Soak the sponges in water and sprinkle a generous layer of grass seed on each sponge. In a week you'll have lush shamrocks.

Patricia Wilmott

Patternmaking

Cut a shamrock pattern from heavy construction paper by folding a square of the paper in half and cutting out a shamrock shape. Use both the shamrock cutout and the piece of paper from which it is cut to make patterns. Place these patterns on a piece of white construction paper. Dip a small square of sponge in water and then into one of the paint squares of a watercolor set. Dab the sponge around the edge of the shamrock or on the inside of the paper from which it was cut for painted patterns. Using a sponge gives the patterns an interesting texture.

Joel A. Nelson

- *A St. Patrick's Day hint: to help children cut out shamrocks, remind them that a shamrock is three hearts together.*

Friends of Old Ireland

The leprechauns of Ireland and Paddy's pig are loved by all children. There is special fun in creating characters who come from the land of fantasy or whimsy. Paddy's pig is an Irish pig, never quite real. Use a paper plate painted green for the body, and cover with shamrocks! Make short, fat leprechauns from short, fat cans, such as those containing small sausages. Trim their green suits with sequin buttons.

Shamrock Puppet

Cut an oak-tag shamrock and color. To add dimension, twist small pieces of green tissue paper around a pencil, then glue twists on shamrock. Attach features and a Popsicle-stick handle.

Eleanor DeJulio

Rainbow Plaques

Have students make St. Patrick's Day plates. Start with paper plates. Each child glues on a yarn rainbow, paints pots of gold and an abundant crop of shamrocks, then adds a cut-paper leprechaun. Tape a yarn loop to the back for hanging.

Ann McCabe

Irish Fun Figures

Modern Irish lads and lassies can wear green calico prints or bits of lace and other findings. Folded green stockings, braided-yarn hair-dos, and cutout shamrocks on pipe-cleaner stems are other inventive touches. Put them all together with clear-drying white glue.

Mary Wilson

Shamrock Prints

Cut a green pepper in half crosswise. Clean out the seeds. Dip the cut edge of the pepper in green paint. Then, using the cut pepper as a stamp, print shamrock designs on a piece of white paper. Overlap shamrocks for a lacy effect, or define them by leaving space between them. Mount the design on green construction paper, leaving room for a border. Shamrock prints make pretty place mats, too.   Mary F. MacDonald

Hats for St. Pat's Day

Each child finds a bowl to fit his or her head. Students dip a sheet of newspaper into liquid-starch water (2 cups starch, 12 cups water) and place it over their molds. Add more sheets. When dry, remove and cut circular brim. Decorate with paint and paper.   Jean Stangl

Irish Dancers

Paddy and wife dance a delightful Irish jig! Color dancers with crayon, using firm strokes. Color in skin and all clothing. Use white crayon for empty spaces. Brush with a thin coat of watery green paint.   Amy West

APRIL

Spring bursts on the scene with bouquets and gardens and baskets of blooms. Springtime creatures peep out from nests and peer down from mobiles. Eggs turn up every way but sunny side up! April crafts are colorful and creative ways to have fun!

Fantastic Flowers

Spring-up your room with colorful garden panels. Overlap construction-paper leaves and flowers. Next, add details in contrasting colors. Use everywhere—in hallways, on bulletin boards, along windows. Or make gigantic blooms—choose a basic shape, build out from the center, and embellish as shown at right. More flowers? Try stenciling. Cut out simple flowers, leaves, butterflies, and ground cover. Use the negatives of the cutouts as stencils. Color onto butcher-block paper until each panel is abloom with great growths of spring.

Helen Evenson

Nesting Time

Create a springlike three-dimensional picture by using plastic egg-carton cups for rounded bird heads. Glue just the edges of the cups to a construction paper background. Cut out and then paste a flat nest shape to the paper. Decorate the birds' "heads" with eyes and beaks. Texture the nest with strips of paper, crisscrossed, gluing down only the ends so they stand out. Add branches and leaves to complete your spring scene.

Judy Irvin

Spring Mobile

Wrap and glue yarn around an embroidery hoop or a ring cut from an oatmeal box. Tie two sets of equal-length yarn to four opposing sides. Knot at top. Attach spring decorations with glue.

Barbara Ellis

Bunny Sacks

Bunny sacks offer a happy solution to the problem of how to carry home all the passed-back papers found during cleanup. They are made from white paper bags (found at drugstore and bakery) and embellished with cut paper, cotton, and paint. They can have taped-on handles, or reinforce bunny's long ears and staple together to form a handle. Either just the face or bunny's entire body may be used in the designing.

Seasonal Weaving

Cut colored construction paper in a 1-inch zigzag pattern in rows across the paper. Make sure that the cuts end about 1/4 inch from the edge. Cut strips of a constrasting color and weave them in and out of the zigzags. Secure with tape. Use another piece of the same size paper and cut out an oval. Place the negative of the mat over your weaving. Carolyn Wilhelm

Bulletin-Board Basket

Arrange and glue plastic-foam pieces in rows to suggest the texture and shape of a big white basket. (Make sure the basket handle is quite tall.) Glue short pieces of yarn around the top of the basket to resemble grass. Have each student decorate a paper egg and glue it in the open space between the grass and the handle. Janice Ford

Springtime Flowers

Flowers don't always have to be small, delicate, and pastel-hued. For a colorful spring bulletin board, make them big, bright, and bold. Note the daisy—it is large enough to have a full-sized paper-plate center. Design other large flowers by combining sections cut from paper plates. Or put together three different-sized plates, after cutting their rims into pointed or scalloped petal shapes.

Plastic sponges, curly gift ribbons, and Styrofoam balls make interesting flower centers. Wire, colored pipe cleaners, or flexible drinking straws can be turned into stamens and pistils. Leave them plain or top with beads, cut-paper shapes, or cotton balls.

Even when flowers are made on a smaller scale, they need not be as intricate as most children try to make them. Around us are many simple objects that already resemble flowers, for example: egg-shell halves, nut cups, plastic picnic spoons and forks, wooden spools, and large coat buttons. Add green leaves and stems, paint, a paper-plate background, small cut-paper insects, and you have a flower plaque!

"Fan"cy Butterflies

Choose bright spring colors of construction paper, and have children fold into various sizes of fan shapes. Cut and shape into butterfly wings. Roll a tube to use for the body. Suspend butterflies from your ceiling or doorways or mount them. Let children experiment with different shapes and layers of color to add interesting plants in the background.   James Perrin

Fold-Open Eggs

Make spring cards from large, fold-open eggs cut from finger-paintings or from paper patterned with string painting. String painting is done by dipping a string in paint and dragging it unevenly across paper. Use two or three different colors.

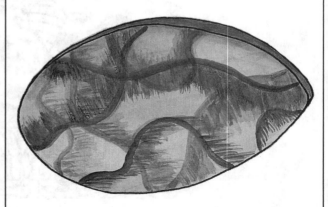

Flower Go 'Round

To create this colorful bouquet you'll need 12- by 18-inch sheets of black construction paper, fabric remnants, and fluorescent paints. First, fashion a vase from the fabric, and glue it near the bottom of the construction paper. Then paint flower stems emerging from the top of the vase. To make flower petals, dip a cylindrical object, such as a cardboard paper-towel tube, into the paint and print circular patterns at the top of the stems.

Joan Mary Macey

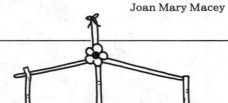

Egg Mobiles

There will be more than just a feeling of spring in the air after you design and hang colorful egg mobiles. Interlock or staple together eight-sided paper egg shapes that have been decorated with swirls of paint (try blowing at puddles of tempera through a paper straw) or cut-paper flowers. Attach thread and hang eggs from coat hangers, doweling, or pieces of basket reed pushed into a Styrofoam ball.

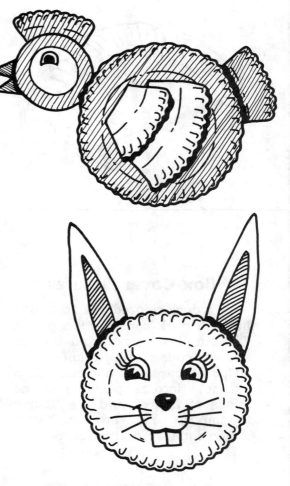

Paper in-the-Round

Too often we forget to give children practice in creating forms that look good from all views—front, back, and sides. These need not always be molded in clay but can be constructed from paper too.

Try designing a paper-plate sculpture to use as a spring centerpiece. The chick's plump body is made from two paper plates joined by stapling their edges together. The head and plate-rim comb and tail are painted on both sides. A section of a plate is taped to each side for wings. Try making a two-faced bunny, asleep on one side, awake on the other.

Paper-Plate Turtle

Turtle from one plate (cut in half) has bead eyes and a flat, cutout head. Add tail and flipper feet.

Box-Cover Pictures

Use a dark-colored box lid or line lid with dark construction paper. Cut bunnies, chicks, and flowers out of construction paper. Cut strips of paper of different sizes and fold into rings. Glue to the backs of figures and the figures to the lid. You have a three-dimensional springtime scene!

Sister Gwen Floryance

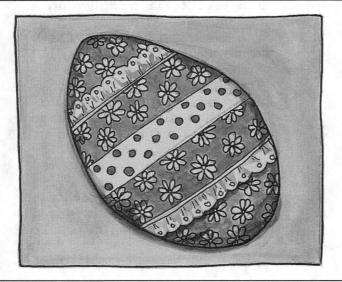

Super-Big Fabric Egg

Each child cuts very large egg shape from small-print material, pads it lightly with polyester fiber, and glues at the very edges to a paper background. Decorations are strips of fabric, lace, ribbon, and so on. Jacqueline Koury

Library Week Bookmarks

Designing original bookmarks in honor of Library Week can be a challenging project when your class tries to think of as many different ways as possible to use a long, narrow strip as an integral part of the whole design. Possibilities are numerous and often humorous. Picture a puppy with a long tongue, a dragon with a forked tail, or a clown falling off a tall ladder.

When putting 3-D trimming on bookmarks, use items such as buttons only on part of the bookmark that sticks out of the book. It is easy to injure the binding of a book by placing too-thick objects between its pages. Thin felt is a good material to use for markers.

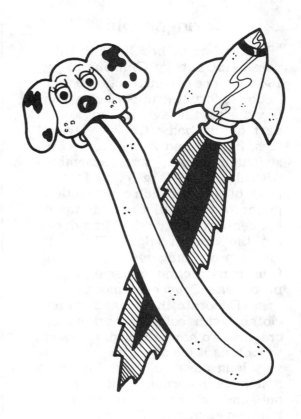

Coat-Hanger Book Rack

Fashion a book rack from one heavy wire coat hanger and a fishing cork. Straighten hanger by pulling at the middle of the bottom bar. Place a pile of several books on the center part of hanger and bend wire around them as shown. Remove wooden peg from cork and slip cork on end of hanger hook. Glue wooden peg back on cork to form beak. Add tack eyes and felt or colored-paper comb and tail. A letter holder can be made from a doll's coat hanger.

- *These are good activities to mark National Library Week.*

Swingpeople

Paint a box or box lid with tempera paint. Let dry. Glue one 12- by 18-inch piece of construction paper to box to form the upper body. The box forms the swing and lower part of the body. Cut two arms, legs, hands, and shoes from construction paper, and assemble with glue. Cut a large circle from a piece of 10- by 10-inch construction paper for the head. Cut a slit up to the center of the circle. Then overlap the circle's edges. This will form a protruding nose. Make hair from construction paper and staple to head. Draw eyes, mouth, and nose. Decorate the swingperson's clothes with colored markers or crayons. To hang the swingperson to look as if it's swinging, cut two very long pieces of yarn. Punch a hole in each corner of the box. Tie one end of string through both holes on each side of the box.

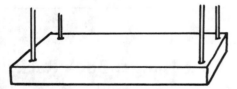

Pull each string evenly to the top of the swingperson. Staple part of the swingperson's body to the string so it will sit upright when hung.
Gail Neu

Stuffed Bunnies

Stuff a colored plastic bag loosely and staple shut. Wrap each of the four corners of the bag tightly with a rubber band. Grab the middle of the bag and carefully wrap a rubber band around it for a head. Glue on eyes, nose, and mouth cut from construction paper. Other possible decorations are ribbons, cotton, and lace.

To make the basket, use a medium-sized brown grocery bag. Cut out a square in the advertisement spot. Draw and write on the basket using pastels, markers, and crayons. Add artificial grass and place bunny inside.
Gail Neu

Bunny Kites

Combine a spring bunny and kites for this fun project. Paint a large bunny body with watercolors on tissue paper. Let dry. Redefine lines with black marker. For bunny's head, fold a 12- by 18-inch piece of construction paper in half. Trace a large circle on it. Cut two circles out. Set one circle aside for back of bunny's head. Draw, color, and cut out facial features, and glue them on the other circle for a face. Draw two ears on a 9- by 12-inch piece of construction paper. Cut out and glue to head. Glue a cardboard strip or stick 28 inches long to head between the ears. The stick should protrude from the bottom of the head. Glue face directly on top of stick and head. Then glue a 15-inch stick horizontally across the bunny body. Center the body on the 28-inch-long stick below the head and glue in place. Add construction paper paws and feet to the body. Attach a long ribbon for the kite's tail. Staple colored tissue paper bows to ribbon for decoration.

Gail Neu

Spring Flowers

Use scraps of paper in the art room to make interesting flower designs. Use plain white paper for the background. Fold, twist, and glue construction-paper scraps into place for the center of the flower. Paint flower petals and stem with tempera paint. Colorful stickers brighten the flower.

Helen Thomas

Shadow-Box Scenes

Reminiscent of the sugar peephole eggs of yesterday, shadow-box scenes should be small and lacy. Use a fluted tidbit plate and build a scene with bits of artificial grass and flowers, tiny cotton chicks and rabbits. (Make your own from cotton colored by dipping it in tempera powder.) These same plates can be given construction-paper sides and handles to make small baskets.

Winged Bird

Students cut a bird body from oak tag or cardboard. Cut a slit in the middle section of the bird's body. Fold two pieces of 9- by 12-inch construction paper accordion-style into fan shapes. Staple one end of each folded fan together. Slip the fans through the slit in the bird's body. Then fold fans slightly out to resemble feathers. Staple the ends of the fan together over the bird's body.

Cartoon Bunnies

Cartooning rabbits is lots of fun. All you do is exaggerate and emphasize the ears, teeth, jaws, and whiskers. Add a humanlike body with enormous feet, or even shoes! Give each bunny a special personality.

Verdie F. Adams

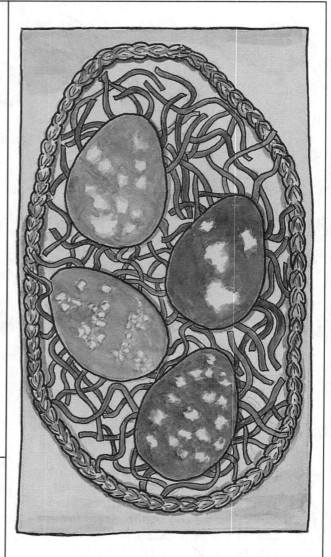

Colorful Egg Nest

Paint several pieces of white paper with a variety of watercolors, one color per piece. While the paint is still damp, sprinkle a pinch of salt over the paper—this will create a marbleized effect. Trace egg shapes on the paper and cut them out. Paste down a small amount of shredded cellophane "grass" on a piece of construction paper and glue the painted eggs on top of it. Use a piece of braided twine for a border. Susan Major Tingey

Easy Baskets

Each child blows up a medium-size balloon, then dips strips of newsprint in starch and covers half of the balloon with several layers of the wet newspaper. When dry, the balloons are popped, leaving sturdy papier-mâché baskets. Cover them with a thin layer of glue and wrap strands of different colored yarn around the baskets. Handles are braided lengths of yarn glued in place.   Kathy Lee

A Tisket, a Tasket

The trick to this pretty basket is taking the time to decorate the paper plate with paints and colored markers first. After children have created colorful patterns to go around the plate, have them lay it flat and fold, following the dotted lines shown. Cut along the solid lines. Fold up into a basket shape, tape or staple.   Jacqueline Koury

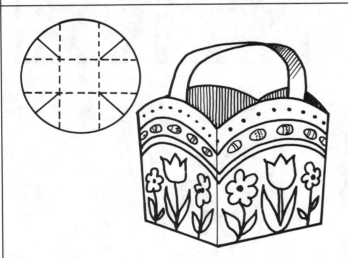

Build a Basket

Cut a 5-inch circle out of cardboard. Cut seven hearts from construction paper. Crease hearts as shown, overlap, and paste together. Stand hearts up and use already-made creases to fold so small curved sections can be pasted underneath the circle, and the rest of the hearts form the "walls" of the basket. Decorate.

Jacqueline Koury

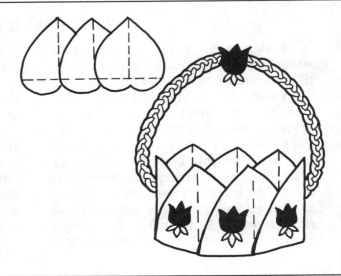

Powder-Puff Faces

Change an inexpensive cotton powder puff into a girl's face smiling beneath a new spring bonnet, made of nearly anything from feathers to lace. Or make a rabbit from a white puff.

Egg Flowers

After children have drawn and filled in egg shapes with bright crayon designs, they cut them out and mount them on cut-paper stems to become modernistic and exotic flowers. June Robb

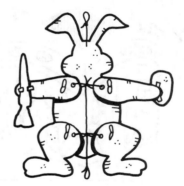

Peter Rabbit Marionette

Cut simple body parts from lightweight cardboard and paint to make this movable rabbit. Length of the body and head is 10 inches; front legs, 4 inches; and back legs, 3½ inches. Punch holes 1/2 inch and 1 inch from the inner ends of the legs. Attach all four legs to the body by inserting brass fasteners through the front into the 1-inch spaced holes. Attach a loop of string through a hole between the rabbit's ears. Then join the top legs with a loop of string tied between the 1/2-inch spaced holes. Repeat with the bottom legs. Using a longer piece of string, knot one end in the center of the loop between the top legs. Tie another loop in the center of the loop between the bottom legs. Let the string hang down about 8 inches and loop the end. Cut out carrots, eggs, or any other objects Peter Rabbit might like to hold in his paws and glue those in place. Move the marionette by pulling top and bottom strings.

Jacqueline Koury

Bizarre Bonnets

Design your own spring hats. To form the top portion, cut a triangle from a paper plate, bring the edges together, and staple. To make a brim, cut away the center section of another plate and attach the remaining ring. Encourage children to experiment with structure, materials, and themes. To make our scorecard hat, mount sports cards on two pieces of cardboard. Form a tent shape for the top of the hat. Rest the scorecard inside. Hang a handy pencil from the brim, and you're ready to go to the game.   Barbara Ellis

Tissue-Paper Collage

You can make a wonderful spring collage with colored tissue paper. First prepare a mixture with equal parts of clear-drying white glue and water. Next, tear a selection of small, irregularly shaped pieces of tissue paper. Arrange the tissue pieces on any background to form an abstract design. Hold each piece in place with one hand, then brush the glue mixture from the center of the piece outward. Overlap the pieces to achieve depth of color. If desired, cut flowers, butterflies, and other spring objects from the finished collage and hang them from strings around the room.

Evelyn Jensen

Animal Pencil Cans

Have children choose a favorite animal. Cut potato-chip can to desired length and decorate with various materials (colored paper, pipe cleaners, bows, and buttons). These are always good gifts.

Vlasta Krieger

FRONT

BACK

Bunny Milk-Jug Baskets

Ask each child to bring in a plastic gallon milk jug from home. Place the jug on a flat surface with the plastic handle portion facing forward. Cut the back half out of the jug directly opposite the handle. Leave approximately 6 inches of plastic along the bottom to form a basket. Students decorate baskets to look like bunnies. The handle forms the bridge of the nose. Have students cut and glue eyes along each side of the handle and a nose and mouth at the bottom of the handle. Staple ears and hair to the top of the jug. Fill the basket with spring grass (sold in drug and discount stores) and goodies for children. These baskets make great holders for spring party treats.   Kathleen Miller

Egg Creatures

Pass around large plastic eggs for students to hold and touch, but not open. Ask students to imagine a creature, ready to hatch, inside the egg. The creature may not be a bird. Give the following directions: Draw the egg shape on a 12- by 18-inch sheet of white drawing paper. Next, draw the creature inside the egg. Add details (eyes, teeth, claws, etc.) and texture (scales, hair, patterns, etc.). Outline everything with marker. Color with colored pencils, crayons, or markers. Color the areas the creature does not fill in a constrasting color. Students cut out egg and mount on construction paper.   Kathleen Schonauer

Dyed Eggs

Everyone loves to dye eggs, even paper ones. Have children draw or trace egg shapes on commercial easy-to-dye paper or hard-surfaced white paper toweling, then decorate with white crayons. If they have trouble using white crayon on white background, have them outline the design first in pencil. They cut out eggs and dip in water-base dye, thinned paint, or a strong solution of food coloring and water. Dye will not penetrate crayoned areas. Joan Lunich Schenk

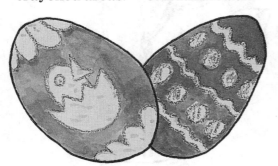

Spring Raindrops

On one side of paper or cardboard raindrop shapes, students put a spring scene, on the other a poem or story. Hang raindrops from different lengths of colored yarn.

Annelle R. Rigsby and Marsha A. Winston

Funny Bunnies

Two plastic coffee cups put together are the basic body shape of these bizarre bunnies. Use rubber cement or special glue for Styrofoam to hold cups together and to add details. Include paper ears, big feet, and cut-paper facial features.

C. A. Carroll

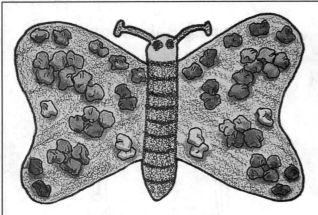

Spring Butterfly

Here's a free-flying crafts idea to make this spring. Trace a large butterfly shape on a piece of tagboard and cut it out. Next, crumple pieces of colored tissue paper into little balls. Glue them onto the tagboard butterfly in a playful pattern. Display butterflies as a group or hang them separately. Lisa Bivona

Trees That Teach

Cut or twist tree shapes and label them to serve as graphic visual aids in any subject. Let leaves represent phonics sounds and use them for drill. Put spelling demons on the leaves, or label leaves to call attention to various subject areas.

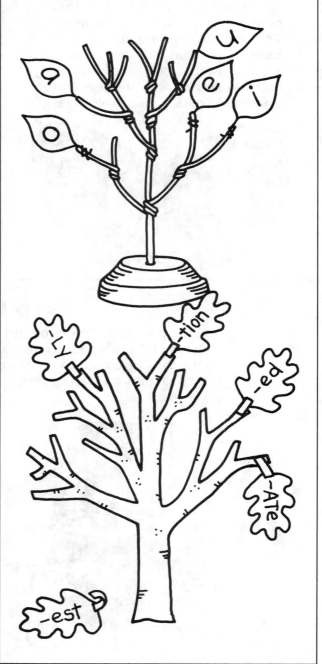

Hand-Print Tree

Cut large tree stump and bare branches from brown paper. Each child makes a print of his or her hand with crayon and adds it to a branch. Jan Benoit

Ming Trees

Make trunk and branches from twisted rolls of brown wrapping paper. Fasten them together with paste-covered strips of the same paper. Anchor the tree in a blob of nonhardening clay or plaster of paris. Cut light and dark green paper into very fine strips. Bunch them together and hold in place by pasting brown paper. At home, children can display trees with clay bases in low bowls with floating flowers.

• *Commemorate Arbor Day by making one of these projects.*

Wallpaper Flowers

Wallpaper samples are useful for stretching a dwindling supply of colored paper and often inspire more creative cut-and-paste designs. Attach colorful flowers to straw or dowel "stems," and plant in sand-filled window boxes.

Joan Lunich Schenk

A Treeful of Birds

Show your class pictures of exotic birds, and discuss their brilliant colors and unique shapes. Have children use bright felt-tipped markers to draw their own birds and then cut them out. Mount on a large tree cut from wood-grained paper. Encourage children to make different-sized birds.

James Perrin

Flower-Petal Designs

Cut a flowerpot out of construction paper, and glue it near the bottom of another piece of construction paper. Flatten out a cardboard tube from a roll of toilet tissue or paper towels. The end of the tube will be petal-shaped. Pass out thick liquid tempera paint on plastic foam meat trays. Students use one end of the tube to make yellow patterns and the other end of the tube to make white patterns. Students fingerpaint the center of the flowers and sponge on green paint for the leaves. Cleanup is quick because you can throw away the meat trays and use sponges to wipe off fingers.   Nancy Wimmer

Kaleidoscope Painting

Fold a square piece of paper in half vertically and then horizontally without unfolding. Next fold the paper in half once diagonally. Unfold. You should have eight sections. Starting closest to the center, paint the same simple shape in the same size and color in each of the eight sections. Radiating out, paint a second set of different shapes, and repeat in each of the sections. Continue radiating from center and repeating different shapes until the paper is filled. The finished design should look like a kaleidoscope.   Susan Major Tingey

Hoppity Express

Imagine how a bunny might deliver his eggs if he were to approach his task as a business. Would he try to create an old-fashioned image by using carts and horses, or fly his hard-boiled cargo in by helicopter? Have children draw their own versions, complete with company logos.
               Ireene Robbins

Bunny Pencil Cup

Cut a bunny from cardboard or heavy construction paper, using construction paper for features. Cut bottom portion from a round plastic bottle. Glue bunny cutout to container with rubber cement.

April Gift Umbrella

April showers bring May flowers and a chance to design pretty umbrellas. Make a dainty parasol by gently folding a tissue-paper-lined circle of colored paper into quarters. Staple the centers of the quarter sections together around a pipe-cleaner handle. Add ribbons and flowers, and tuck sticks of gum or pieces of candy into the folds of the parasol.

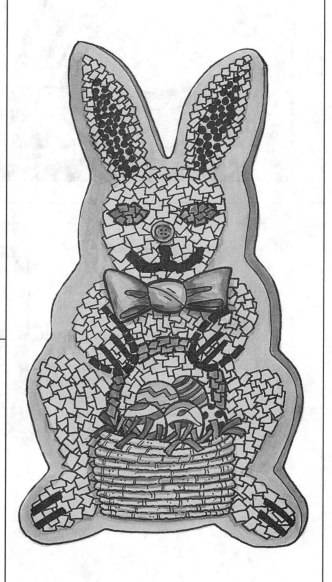

Springtime Cards

Fluffy, woolly, fuzzy things just naturally seem a part of springtime. Glue bits of tissue paper and yarn, wood shavings, ravelings from soft fabrics, crushed egg shells, shredded rubber or plastic foam, etc. on fold-over animal- and bird-shaped cards.

Springtime Frogs

Frogs are symbols of spring just as flowers are, and they can make marvelous subjects for drawings and paintings, too. If possible, "borrow" a live model for your class. Tell children not to copy the frog but to observe its outstanding characteristics.

James Perrin

Spring Garden

Cut contact paper into twelve 1/4-inch strips and one 1/2-inch strip. Affix strips to white construction paper to resemble a picket fence. Then, using a sponge, dab pastel watercolors on and around the fence. Let dry. Remove contact paper—outline of fence remains. Add details with dark-colored markers or watercolors. The fence stencil can be reused several times.

Susan Major Tingey

Rainy-Day Scenes

Have children draw simple rainy-day scenes with crayons—perhaps a self-portrait of the artist holding a colorful umbrella or wearing a bright yellow slicker. The sky and most of the background is left blank. Then students draw rain with blue watercolor markers (Crayola gives best results). When the picture is dipped in clear water, raindrops "run." Dry on newspapers.

Sister Gwen Floryance

MAY

Woven, pasted, or sewn, May baskets hold flowers of many hues, textures, and materials. Cookie cutters, milk cartons, wallpaper samples, and dry pasta are just some of the ingredients of this crafty month.

Celebrate Mother's Day with cards, banners, bookmarks, and other gifts. Decorate year-end classrooms with class memory quilts and delicate flower chains.

May Garlands

Brighten your classroom or hallways with these blossoming garlands. Cut the cups out of pastel-colored Styrofoam egg cartons and fray the edges with scissors. Fit three different-colored cups inside each other for multicolored flowers. Using a needle and a long double strand of yarn, string the cups together into a garland. Make a knot at the bottom of each flower to prevent slipping. Staple or glue bows cut from construction paper onto the garland between each flower. Or, for a variation, cut the bottoms of the cups and glue to bows like a daffodil.   Julie Stempinski

Goldfish Aquarium

Color a white plastic-foam meat tray in various shades of blue and green using colored markers. Make underwater plants from green and yellow paper, and glue along the bottom edge. Bend a thin piece of wire into a fishing hook shape. Cut a worm from construction paper, and attach to the hook. Push the hook through the top lip of the meat tray to look as if someone is fishing. Add goldfish crackers, either glued down or loose for a swimming effect. Cover tray with cellophane, and stretch it tight across the front. Secure cellophane in back with tape.

Christie Costanzo

Flowery May Basket

Fold large piece of colorful paper in half and draw the outline of a flower on one half, keeping paper folded. Cut out to get two flower shapes. Paste or sew the shapes together, leaving top open. Add green stems and leaves. Two twisted strands of yarn make a handle stapled to flower top.

Marilyn Karns

Pop-Bottle Sculptures

Each student brings a small (8- to 10-inch) soft drink bottle to school to use as an armature. Students drape the bottle with one or two layers of cheesecloth to prevent clay from sticking to it. They wrap the bottle with two ½-inch-thick slabs of clay cut from a large block. The children use moistened fingertips or sponges to smooth joints between clay slabs. Students should not smooth the clay down, as it leaves the top too thin.

The clay-covered bottle is a basic column around which students form their sculpture. They add clay to form shoulders, muzzles, lips, tails and so on. Students can add secondary figures, such as a ball player carrying a bat and glove.

Once the clay dries, remove the bottle, leaving a hollow, freestanding sculpture that is ready for the kiln. After firing, paint sculptures with acrylic paint and layer with protective shellac.

Laura Revness and Michael Brozda

Paper-Bag May Baskets

Every child should have the pleasure, at least once, of hanging a pretty May basket of flowers on someone's doorknob. Make baskets small, so that only a few flowers will be needed.

Cut sides of a paper bag into strips and weave around them with pieces cut from a second bag or from colored paper.

Make a folded-paper decoration to trim the basket's top by placing the ends of two narrow paper strips (same length and width) at right angles to one another, and folding each one, in turn, over the other. Paste the completed length of expandable squares around the basket top, after a pipe-cleaner or cord handle has been added.

For stronger baskets, place one bag inside another, pasting the bottom of the inner bag in place. Cut and weave around only the outer bag.

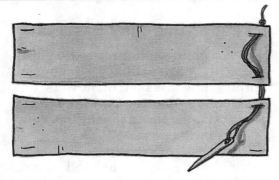

Venetian-Blind Paintings

Paint a spring picture on a piece of paper any desired color or size. Let dry. Outline the picture with black marker. Cut the paper into several horizontal panels, making sure panels are of equal width. Cut two slits in the end of each panel. Then sew panels together, leaving space between each one so the finished product looks like a Venetian blind. To do this, cut two pieces of yarn longer than the picture. Thread one piece of yarn through the first slit in the first panel, knot it, and continue threading yarn through each slit in every panel in an over-under fashion. Knot yarn at bottom. Then thread other side of panels.

Gail Neu

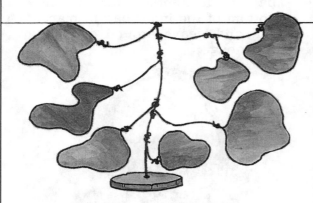

See-Through Sculpture

Use pliers to twist strong but pliable wire into large loops of varying sizes. Wire used to band together newspapers is excellent, and free. Push loops into interesting forms with fingers and squeeze glue onto wire. Lay pieces of colored tissue paper on the glue. After glue is dry, trim away excess paper and paint or spray with varnish.

James Perrin

Beautiful Butterflies

Give younger children a pattern for tracing a butterfly on two different colors of paper. They cut them out and decorate with geometric paper shapes. The two pieces are glued together in the middle and two wings folded up for a 3-D effect.

Sarah Pla

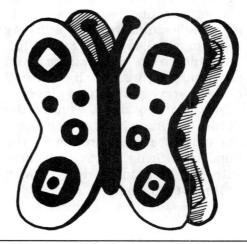

Clown Banks

Papier-mâché clown heads make happy banks. Cover cans with layers of paste-soaked paper. Build individual features such as noses and bulging eyes from wads of paper or taped-on bottle caps. Remove both ends of cans and cover with the pasted paper. Paint with tempera. Money slots are cut in the tops. Bottoms can be broken for "withdrawals," then a new bottom made. Marianne Seehafer

Color Waves

Children will love this easy abstract art. Have students use 8½- by 11-inch sheets of construction paper in colors they like seeing together. Cut 11-inch lengths of wavelike shapes out of at least five different sheets and overlap in an interesting presentation. Let students experiment and share their effects. Joan Lunich Schenk

Zoo Animals

Who's looking at whom in this zoo? These animals' heads will bob gently as they gaze at all who come to admire them. To make, children draw and cut out heads of their four-footed favorite friends. Now make a folded-paper fence long enough to cover all the animals, and staple its ends to a backdrop of blue sky or green grass. Attach each head to one side of a stapled ring of paper; then paste the opposite side of the ring to the backdrop above the fence. This is a good follow-up activity to a zoo, farm, or circus trip. Beatrice Bachrach Perri

• *This is a good project for National Pet Week too!*

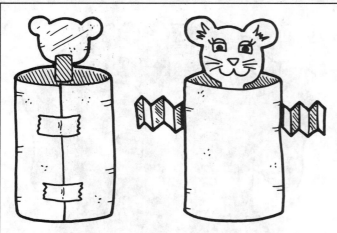

Paper-Cylinder Hand Puppet

Tape the short ends of a 9- by 12-inch sheet of construction paper together to make a cylinder. Cut a face and hair from another piece of paper and paste on top front of cylinder. Strips of paper folded accordion-style are attached to body as arms. Put hand into cylinder to move puppet.

A Furry Friend

Introduce simple sewing techniques to your students with this mouse puppet. Cut a 4-inch circle from fake-fur fabric. Fold the circle in half, fur sides together, and sew the curved edge shut. Cut a 1-inch slit at one end of the fold and turn the mouse furry side out. Add a tail, nose, ears, and eyes of your choice. Put your index finger in the slit, and move your furry friend about!

Mary Ann Panko

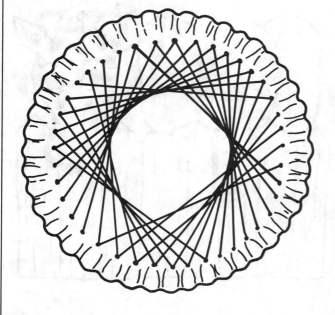

String Arounds

Paper plates with ribbed rims make ideal backgrounds for string designs. Have students use the ribbing to guide the even spacing of holes poked around the inside of the rim with a blunt needle. Children thread this same needle with any colored heavy thread. They start at one point and cross the plate to another, perhaps 15 to 20 holes away. From this hole, they return to the second hole, and go from there to the 16th or 21st. Once a pattern is developed, students continue until the design is around the plate. They go around in opposite direction.

Ireene Robbins

Broken-Crayon Creations

Use small pencil sharpeners to shave broken crayons. Put each color in a separate egg-carton cup. Lay heavy newspaper padding on top of an ironing board or other suitable surface. Cover the base of a flatiron with heavy foil, folding it up around the sides. Set the temperature at medium, steam off. Have students tear waxed paper into 18- by 24-inch sheets and fold each in half. Each child sprinkles 1/4 teaspoon of several colors of shavings between the waxed paper. An adult irons the creations until the shavings melt and blend and paper edges are sealed. When cool, mount them in construction-paper frames.   Emma Ruth Henry

Be a Clown

Your students will love to turn themselves into a bunch of clowns. Begin by making a silhouette of each child. In turn, place children between light from a projector and sheets of manila or oaktag. Trace around the shadows of the faces. Children cut out their silhouettes and then cut an extra one from manila paper. With pieces of construction paper, crayons, and felt-tipped markers, they turn one of their profiles into a unique clown head. Display the two silhouettes side by side, for others to admire and to compare.   Rosemary McCoskey

Calico Butterflies

Cotton fabric, thread-covered wire, pipe cleaner, glue, and a small magnet make this butterfly to decorate a refrigerator or file cabinet for Mother's Day. Cut a butterfly shape from two contrasting pieces of cloth. Lay one piece wrong side up and glue on two pieces of wire (one from upper right to lower left wing, the other in the opposite direction) to make an X shape. Fold a longer piece of wire in half, bend to form antennae, and glue along center of butterfly. Spread glue on the other cloth shape and press on top of the first, matching edges. Glue a pipe-cleaner piece down center of one side to make body, and a flat magnet on the opposite side. When dry, bend wings and antennae into shape. Spray with acrylic clear fixative.

Dianne C. Powell

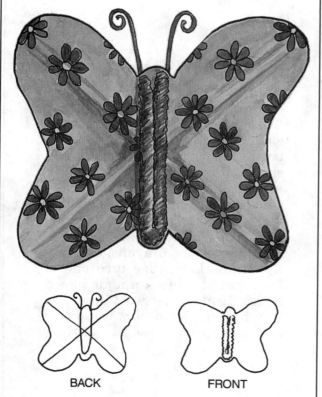

BACK   FRONT

Mother's Day Banner

A banner present for Mother's Day is this happy little hanging. Select cloth or colored construction paper in springtime colors. Choose motifs that are simple but fit a spring theme, too. Put together with white glue. Hang with yarn.

Julia Henry

Mother's Day Potpourri

Spread flower petals on old window screens so air can circulate around them. When dry, mix 6 to 8 cups with 1 t. nutmeg, 1 T allspice, 1 T cloves, 3 T cinnamon, 2 T powdered orris root, 5 to 10 drops rose oil (or any perfumed oil). Store a week in dark place, shaking now and then. Tie 1/4 cups in 6-inch cloth squares.   Marilyn Karns

Mother's Day Gifts

Mix 2 cups baking soda, 1 cup cornstarch, and 1¼ cup cold water. Knead the mixture until it's malleable. Design pendants, paperweights, even belt buckles. Let dry for a day, paint, and shellac.

Rosie Williams

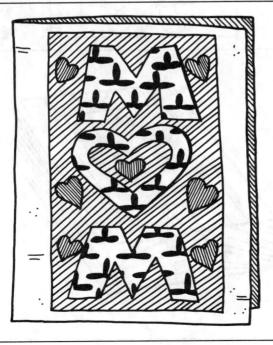

Mother's Day Card

Use material scraps to make Mother's Day cards. First cut out the letters *M O M* from fabric. Make the *O* a heart. Glue the fabric letters to complementary colors of construction paper for backing. Trim away the paper, leaving a thin border. Cut little hearts from the paper scraps, and glue the letters and hearts to a folded sheet of paper. Write your message inside.

James Perrin

- *Celebrate Mother's Day by making a special gift or card.*

Mother's Day Bookmark Card

Fold cardboard inserts from pantyhose in half lengthwise and write greeting inside. From tagboard cut a flower with a long stem and leaves. Color both sides. Cut two slits in the card front and insert the stem. Mother can remove flower for a bookmark.   H. Marcin

Gift-Card Combination

Gift and card combine in this light-hearted Mother's Day present. Crayon a figure on the card and pull corners of a print handkerchief through slits in card for a colorful apron and kerchief.

Wooden Paperweight

After the piece of wood is sawed and sanded, apply the first coat of varnish. (Leave bottom plain.) When dry, sand lightly and give second coat. While varnish is still "tacky" press on a small photo of child. Brush last coat of varnish over photo and wood. Glue felt to base. A fine Mother's Day gift!

Gift for Mother

To make an attractive, sturdy shopping bag, use gummed paper tape (like that used to wrap postal packages) to reinforce a heavy brown grocery sack. Tape the bottom inside seams of the bag. Then fold 3 inches of the top edge to the inside and tape. Staple on pieces of clothesline rope or strong cord to make handles. Cover staples with tape.

Cut design from colored paper or fabric and attach with wallpaper paste.

Weavings

Collect colorful yarn. Have children weave into slotted paper plates or pizza liners. Decorate the inside with a photograph, a favorite poem, saying, or wish. These are wonderful Mother's Day gifts.

Jacqueline Armin

Sunshine Card

Paste together four 9-inch circles of white construction paper and cut points out along the edge. While the paste is still wet, mold the center over a jar lid. Let the figure dry as a three-dimensional form. Paint your molded sun with warm colors. Use as a Mother's Day card with the message "You light up my life!"   Joan Mary Macey

Pretty Plaque

Cut center design from thick cardboard or paper. Paint motif and plate rim with metallic paint. (Copper is especially good-looking.) Glue motif to plate by pasting a piece of sponge between paper design and plate. Use gummed hanger.

Filigree Fish

Have children cut undersea shapes from black paper, cutting out the inside of each shape in a filigree-type pattern. Let students practice their watercolor-wash techniques, shading paper to look like they imagine it would look underwater. Mount shapes on their favorite background, then display.

James Perrin

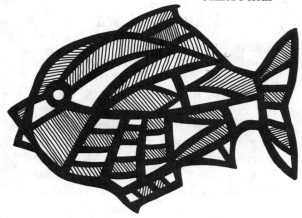

Full-Size Dolls

Make a pal that's just your size. For this project you'll need a discarded bed sheet. First double it, then lie down on it, and have someone trace around you with a felt-tip marker, keeping the line a few inches from your body. Don't worry about small details like fingers and toes. Carefully use straight pins to pin the halves smoothly in place and then cut the figure out with a sharp scissors (your cutting line should be a few inches from your outline). With a needle and thread carefully stitch on the outline, leaving an open space somewhere for stuffing. Remove the pins, turn the doll inside out, and stuff with rags or foam. (Don't use newspaper for stuffing; it is very flammable.) If you keep your stuffing pieces small, your doll won't be as lumpy. When it's all stuffed, sew the opening together. Decorate the doll any way you'd like: use markers, dress it in your clothes, or embroider features on it. You can even make a whole family with pets!

Paper-Bag Hand Puppets

These puppets are simple and fun to make. Remember that the mouth opening always falls on the fold of the bag, so that the underside of the flap is the inside of the mouth. Add features with interesting materials, perhaps real straw to create a scarecrow.

Popsicle Boxes

Glue 11 Popsicle sticks together to make a flat base. To build sides, glue one stick to the edge of the base. Rotate, and glue another stick so that sides overlap at the corners log-cabin fashion. Make a flat lid using 11 more sticks, then decorate.

Barbara Kramer

Chromatography Butterflies

Mix red, yellow, and blue food colors together. Cut coffee filters into butterfly shapes, wet, and drip on the color mixture. Colors will spread and separate. Some colors' molecules are heavier than others' so the water carries colors at different speeds to create this spectrum.

Judith Reichbach

Litter Bags

Decorate with whimsical "scatter-pillars," "trashoppers," or the more common "litterbugs." Use bits of real trash as part of insect's design. Give it match-stick legs, a gum-wrapper body, toothpick feelers, or torn newspaper wings. Glue these extra touches firmly to the bag and draw the rest of the insect with markers or crayons. Don't forget to letter the name below.

Closet Freshener

Poke holes in two clean sour cream cups. Fill one cup with potpourri or cloves, and glue on other cup. Decorate with yarn and felt.

Anna Lee

Works of Art

This quick art idea will give students' imaginations a real workout. Cut pictures of people, animals, or objects from discarded magazines, trimming each one carefully. Distribute two pictures to each child, choosing pairs that appear as unrelated as possible, along with plain white paper. Students paste both pictures on the paper in any positions they want, then use crayons to draw larger pictures incorporating them. When done, magazine pictures should blend into their surroundings.

Pamela Klawitter

Wheelless Wagon

Take a 9- by 12-inch sheet of paper. Fold all sides up 1¾ inches and make two cuts on opposite ends (four cuts) from edge of paper to fold lines. Overlap tabs and paste to form box. Draw, color, and cut out figures of a child and pet. Fold to sitting positions and paste in wagon. Tape a 36-inch length of string or yarn along bottom and up front end of wagon. Little children love this!

Beatrice Bachrach Perri

A De"light"ful Gift

These candlesticks are easy to make and fun to give. Start with empty wooden spools of thread—all sizes are fine. Use about three or four for each candlestick. Let students arrange and glue together. At the top, glue a screw-on cap from a 3-liter soft-drink bottle. This will hold the candle. Now choose various pasta shapes to glue onto the candlestick. The result is a great natural look. Try spray painting.

James Perrin

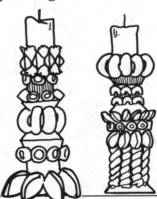

Triple-Layered Designs

A pair of pointed scissors and three sheets of the same size (but different colors) of construction paper will produce open designs with a layered look. Students poke or stab into each sheet of paper at random and cut out interesting shapes. They can use straight-lined shapes or curved-line shapes or a combination of both. Be sure they poke into the paper and not cut in from the edges. When substantial areas have been removed from each piece, stack all three sheets together and staple. Add a fourth sheet for backing if you desire.

Joan Mary Macey

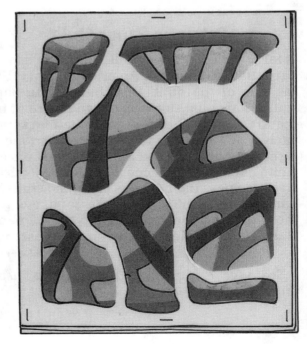

Winged Beauty

Fold one full sheet of dark-colored tissue paper in half. Use chalk to draw the outline of half a butterfly, and cut out latticework-type designs inside the wings. Open your butterfly carefully and flatten it on a large plastic garbage bag. Brush with a solution of one part white glue to two parts water. Fill in the latticework with scraps of bright tissue paper, brushing them with the glue mixture. (Colors will probably run, but that's even prettier!) Let the butterfly dry overnight. Then peel it carefully from the plastic and let the sun shine through!

Regina Cabral

Animal Quilts

Each child cuts an animal outline from a wallpaper sample and pastes it on contrasting paper. Tear edges to make it irregular. With black crayon, draw animals' features and trace stitching patterns around outlines and along edges of backgrounds. Finished pictures are pinned on a sheet. Hang to display class quilt.

Helen Wubbenhorst

Patriotic Paper Quilt

Make a class paper quilt to add a dash of patriotism to a unit on American history. Plan the size of the quilt. Distribute white paper squares of equal size to each student to fit into the area. Distribute red and blue markers to each child. Students must plan a patriotic design using only the red and blue markers and white background. Some ideas for designs are stars, stripes, and patterns using the students' names. When the designs are complete, glue them together on one large piece of paper. Hang in a prominent place in the classroom.

Dee Le Fevour

• See page 70 for source materials to inspire other quilt projects.

Crazy Headbands

Purchase narrow, soft plastic headbands. Before distributing to children, make two holes in tops of bands with a sharp object, such as a point of a compass. Make springy wire by wrapping florist's wire around a pencil into a spiral shape. Attach one end of each spiral wire through the holes in the headband. Students make fun designs to attach to ends of spiral wires for antennae. Plastic foam balls, pipe cleaners, and glitter add to the wild look. Let students wear their antennae during physical education for added fun.

Alice Crouse and Nancy Ziegenbein

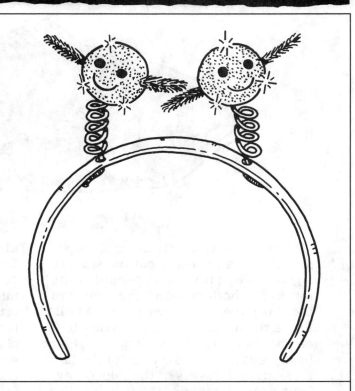

Cooky-Cutter Craft

A quick, easy-to-do art project! Children trace around cutters to get a basic animal shape, then decorate it as they wish. A paper punch can provide spots. Leftover tape makes fine stripes. Put some animals in paper cages and tie yarn reins on others.

Milk-Carton Lanterns

Instead of May baskets, children might like to make flowery milk-carton lanterns. Slit milk-carton sides or cut "windows" from carton and push down gently on its roof to shape the sides. Paste on cut-paper flowers, birds, or butterflies and colored paper to decorate lantern. Attach a yarn handle.

Grocery-Bag Fish

Make a colorful fish using a paper grocery bag. To begin, cut the sides of a grocery bag from the opening at the top to the bottom along the center of the side panel. Fold the cut bag in half. Trace the outline of a fish on one half of the bag. Then, holding the bag firmly, cut along the outline of the fish through both layers of the folded bag. Glue around edges of the fish, leaving about 6 inches unglued at the belly. Decorate the fish with colored construction-paper scales, glitter, marker, etc. Stuff the fish with crumpled newspaper through the bottom of the belly. Then glue the belly closed. Hang fish from the ceiling with a piece of nylon fishing line.

Joel A. Nelson

Silhouette Flowers

Fold a 9-inch square of black construction paper in half. Sketch a half circle and cut it out. Back the hole with clear contact paper. Cut out petals and stems for flowers from the circle. Arrange shapes and design on contact paper.

Back with cellophane paper and use as a spring window decoration.

Susan Major Tingey

Butterfly Mobiles

Cut four pairs of butterfly wings from cardboard, decorate front and back, and sandwich each pair of wings between two ice-cream sticks with paste. Paste a wire twist-em to the top end of each set of sticks for antennae. Use yarn, glued to the center of each butterfly, for hanging.

Jane K. Priewe

Tape Mural

Want a unique way to summarize a book, film, or class outing? Have students work as a class to illustrate a story or event using adding machine tape and markers or crayons. Each student chooses a particular subject to illustrate. When the entire tape is unrolled, it tells a picture story, much like a filmstrip!

Barbara Ellis

Hummingbird Feeder

Have children bring in a clean plastic bottle. (Rounded bottles work best.) The teacher should heat an ice pick and punch several holes around the bottle 3 inches from the bottom. Wrap a piece of thin wire around the bottle neck for hanging purposes. (Ants will crawl on string, so wire is best.) To make hummingbird food, boil a mixture of 1/2 cup of sugar and 1/2 cup of water. Let cool. Add a few drops of red food coloring. Add liquid to feeder, making sure liquid level is not above holes. Hang on a tree out of reach of animals and enjoy watching hummingbirds feed all summer long.

Grace Gannon

Art Attachés

For each carryall, you'll need a piece of heavy fabric, like denim, about 2 feet by 1½ feet. Help kids lay the material flat, right side down, so the shorter side is at the bottom. Fold up 9 inches and stitch to form sides. Fold remaining material down to overlap. Attach with Velcro strips. Decorate.

Penny Carter

Class Memories

Students can create hangings of class memories. Each child has a square or long strip of cotton muslin. Help him or her to mark it off into several equal areas. Children then ask friends to decorate each area by drawing something in crayon about themselves or about the school year and sign their names. When the banner is completed, an adult presses it carefully on the wrong side to set colors. A hem is stitched at the top, a dowel inserted, and a cord added for hanging.   Esther Heisey

Floral Notes

Press flowers between paper towels inside a heavy book. Leave for several days. Glue small arrangements onto colored tissue paper. Mount on construction paper cards. Press again.   Celeste Conway

Wax-Paper Butterflies

Waxen-winged butterflies accent the artful blending of colors on butterfly wings. To achieve this effect, scatter crayon shavings between two sheets of wax paper and press with a warm iron. Cut butterfly shapes, fold across the middle, and fit into clip-clothespin bodies. Add pipe-cleaner antennae.

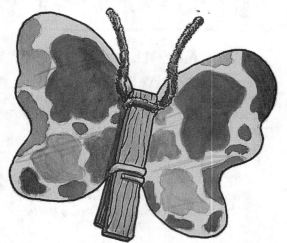

Summer Foods

Foods for summer are special. The opening of the local ice cream or hot dog stand is often a long-awaited event for children. Let them depict their favorite warm-weather treat using paper, fabric, yarn, and wallpaper samples. Foods will have a brand-new look!

Joan Lunich Schenk

Treat Plate

Make a pretty cookie-passing plate for end-of-year parties by using a dipped-and-dyed paper coffee filter. For dye, use food colorings diluted with a little water. Fold the filter into halves, quarters, or eighths, then dip the different sections in the dyes. Open carefully and let dry. Now refold and cut out designs "snowflake style." Place the completed "doily" on a paper plate, brush with liquid starch, dry, and you're ready to serve!

Margaret Kolak

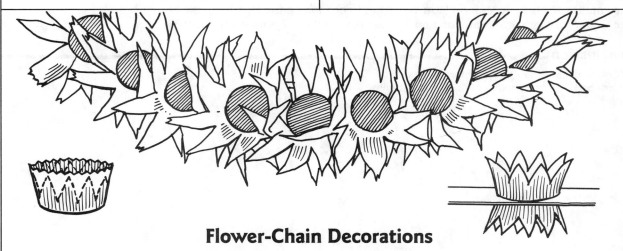

Flower-Chain Decorations

Chains of flowers can add a charming, slightly old-fashioned air to end-of-year ceremonies.

Attach flowers to lengths of rickrack, yarn, or narrow ribbon. To make a double-daisy chain, use cupcake liners. Each blossom takes four liners, two on each side of chain. Cut sides of liners into petals, glue liners together, staple to chain; paste on centers to cover staples.

Resources

Collage

Source materials to use with collage projects:
Pictures of the work of Romare Bearden, Arthur Dove, Joseph Cornell, Henri Matisse, and Kurt Schwitters
Picture books illustrated by Leo Leonni and Ezra Jack Keats

Paper Folding

Books that include other paper-folding projects:
Elementary Art Games and Puzzles by Florence Temko (Parker/Prentice-Hall, 1982)
Paper Dreams by Lorraine Bodger (Universe Books, 1977)
Papercrafts by Ian Adair (David and Charles Holdings, Ltd., 1975)

Color

A sourcebook on personal interpretation of color:
The Art of Color by Yohannes Itten (Van Nostrand Reinhold, 1973)
To expand color awareness:
Pictures of the work of Paul Gaugin, Claude Monet, Georgia O'Keeffe, Pierre-Auguste Renoir, and Vincent Van Gogh

Art Activities to Help Children Communicate

Tell Me About Your Picture: Art Activities to Help Children Communicate by Janet Carson (Prentice-Hall, 1984)

Quilting

To inspire other quilting projects:
Nonfiction
Great American Quilts (Oxmoor House, 1988)
The Complete Book of Patchwork Quilting and Appliqué by Linda Seward (Prentice-Hall, 1987)
101 Patchwork Patterns by Ruby McKim (Dover, 1962)
The Standard Book of Quilt Making and Collecting by Marguerite Ickis (Dover, 1949)
Fiction
The Josefina Story Quilt by Eleanor Coerr (Harper & Row, 1986)
The Keeping Quilt by Patricia Polacco (Simon and Schuster Books for Young Readers, 1988)
The Patchwork Quilt by Valerie Flournoy (Dial Books for Young Readers, 1985)
The Quilt Story by Tony Johnston and Tomie dePaola (G. P. Putnam's Sons, 1985)

Imagination

A book of visual poems by a painter:
Sounds by Wassily Kandinsky (Yale University Press, 1980)

Index